What Is Vocation?

Basics of the Faith

How Do We Glorify God?
How Our Children Come to Faith
What Are Election and Predestination?
What Is a Reformed Church?
What Is a True Calvinist?
What Is Biblical Preaching?
What Is Church Government?
What Is Justification by Faith Alone?
What Is Perseverance of the Saints?
What Is Providence?
What Is Spiritual Warfare?
What Is the Christian Worldview?
What Is the Lord's Supper?
What Is True Conversion?
What Is Vocation?
Why Do We Baptize Infants?

What Is Vocation?

Stephen J. Nichols

P&R
PUBLISHING

P.O. BOX 817 • PHILLIPSBURG • NEW JERSEY 08865-0817

Scripture quotations are from *ESV Bible* ® (*The Holy Bible, English Standard Version* ®). Copyright © 2001 by Crossway Bibles, a publishing ministry of Good News Publishers. Used by permission. All rights reserved.

Page design by Tobias Design

Library of Congress Cataloging-in-Publication Data

Nichols, Stephen J., 1970-
  What is vocation? / Stephen J. Nichols.
    p. cm. -- (Basics of the faith)
  Includes bibliographical references.
  ISBN 978-1-59638-177-3 (pbk.)
  1. Vocation--Christianity. 2. Work--Religious aspects--Christianity.
I. Title.
  BV4740.N53 2010
  248.8'8--dc22

2010006412

■ **Two quite disparate** groups of people have something profoundly interesting to say about work: the Reformers and country-music singers. Who can forget Dolly Parton's song "9 to 5," now thirty years old? All she can do, in the lyrics of the song, is dream about a better life; for now she just laments the day-in-day-out work. It's 9 to 5 today, 9 to 5 tomorrow, and weeks ahead of 9-to-5 days. And for all that, Parton laments that she's only "barely getting by."

More contemporary audiences can sing along to Alan Jackson's "Good Time." You can hear the drudgery in his voice when he painfully ekes out, "Work, work, all week long." The only bright spot for him is the weekend. Free of work, free of the boss, free of the time clock, he can have a "Good Time." He longs for it so much, he even spells out the words G-O-O-D and T-I-M-E in the song.

Work songs have been around as long as there has been work, at least in American contexts. Slaves sang about the hardships of work in the spirituals. At the turn of the twentieth century, railroad work crews or cotton-picking sharecroppers passed the time by singing "work hollers," sounding off to each other as a means of surviving brutal conditions. And the beat goes on to this day. Not only in country music, but in nearly all other styles of American music, work gives cause for lament.

5

The workweek is to be endured, with temporary reprieves coming on the weekends, the precious few weeks of vacation, and the fleeting years of retirement. If you listen to most music, you'll find that work gets a bad rap. And the music is a mere symptom of the culture, especially American culture. In any given survey, high statistics reveal that few among us find fulfillment, let alone dignity, in work. In contrast, try an Internet search for the word *vacation*. Last time I did, I had hits in the millions.

But next to country singers, another group has something to say about the subject of work. This group of people is the Reformers, and they have a lot to say about work. In fact, they prefer a different word for it: *vocation*. This word means "calling," instantly filling the notion of work with purpose, meaning, fulfillment, dignity, and even happiness. In the hands of the Reformers work is transformed, or re-formed, back to a place and a position in which God intended it to be.

Given the cultural climate concerning work, we would be well served by some historical, theological, and biblical reflections on work. Add up the hours, the weeks, the months, and the years; work fills the lion's share of our lives. Certainly God has not left us in the dark when it comes to work. In the pages of this booklet, we'll explore what Scripture teaches concerning work. We'll also look at how the Reformers shaped those teachings into the doctrine of vocation. Finally, we'll see what this doctrine of vocation means for us in the twenty-first century.

For many, Dolly Parton's line that we're "just a step on the boss-man's ladder" rings all too true when it comes to work. How sad, when a line from the psalmist declares a rather different notion: "Let the favor of the Lord our God be upon us, and establish the work of our hands upon us; yes, establish the work of our hands!" (Ps. 90:17).

That's the vision of work we all want. And to get it, we need to understand this word *vocation*. So we'll begin with the question: What is vocation? Try an Internet search for the word. Last time I did, I found more hits than I thought I would—but far, far fewer hits than for *vacation*. We plan and think (and dream) about our vacations, but we should also apply at least a little energy to thinking about vocation.

DEFINING *VOCATION*

Latin lesson time. The English word *vocation* comes from the Latin word *vocatio* or, in the verb form, *vocare*. Its root means "calling." It appears that William Tyndale, in his English translation of the Bible, first used the word in English. All Tyndale did was to bring the Latin word directly over into the English language. This Latin word that Tyndale transliterated into English had a technical and specific meaning. For a time, leading up to Luther, people had applied this Latin word nearly exclusively to church work. Priests, nuns, monks—they each had a calling. Everyone else in medieval culture, from merchants to peasants, from nobles to knights, simply worked.

Previously, however, in the Middle Ages, this hadn't always been the case. Especially in the early days of monasticism and in several monastic orders, work was viewed with dignity. *Ora et Labora* was their motto. Translated, this phrase means "Pray and work" (Latin lesson 2). Monks also knew how to reward themselves after their work. They invented, among other things, the pretzel, which came from a Latin word meaning "gift," and more specifically "small gift." Pretzels were the little rewards that monks enjoyed and passed on to children after the completion of a hard task, once the duties were done. They placed value on work and they placed value on play and leisure. Many of these monks recognized work as one of the good gifts from the gracious hand of God.

At this point, we need to clarify the use of the words *work* and *vocation*. The word *work* can be used narrowly to refer to your job for which you get paid. Or it may be used more broadly, as in: "Mowing grass on a hot August day is hard work." *Vocation* too can be used to refer to a specific calling, or used more broadly to refer to all of one's life.

Work and *vocation* can sometimes be used interchangeably, while at the same time they can mean two quite different things. The aim of this booklet is to show the connections between the terms. In fact, it's the goal of this booklet for you to see all of your work, whether you get a paycheck for it or not, whether it's considered a noble profession or a menial task, as germane to your calling as a child of God and a disciple of Christ.

Now back to the monks and the Middle Ages. By the latter centuries of the Middle Ages, roughly the 1200s to the 1500s, work had fallen out of favor. It was viewed as a lesser thing, as merely putting in time. Those who had callings were exclusively in the direct service of the church.

The Reformers challenged many practices and beliefs of latter medieval Roman Catholicism. Here we trot out the solas: *sola Scriptura* (Scripture alone); *sola gratia* and *sola fide* (salvation by grace alone through faith alone); *solus Christus* (Christ alone); and *soli Deo gloria* (for the glory of God alone). This last one, *soli Deo gloria*, factors in to our discussion. Playing off this idea, Martin Luther gave new life, extensive and broad life, to the word *vocation*. He applied the word to being a spouse, a parent, or a child. He applied the word to the various professions.

Granted, the professions were limited in the 1500s, not nearly approaching the types of specializations we have today. But doctors, lawyers, merchants—these were all vocations, callings. (One profession that Luther didn't care much for was banking, but that's for another time.) Luther also applied vocation to the work of the peasant class, to the farmers and servants. To Luther, all work and all the roles that we play were potentially holy callings, which could be fulfilled for the glory of God alone.[1]

A few generations later, another German Lutheran, Johann Sebastian Bach, illustrated Luther's teaching perfectly. Whether Bach was writing music commissioned by and for the church or whether it was for other purposes, he signed all his music with two sets of initials: one for his name, and the other, "SDG," for *Soli Deo Gloria*. All work—all types of work, not just the work done in the service of the church—was a calling.

We can be quite grateful to the Reformers for making a number of contributions to Christian beliefs and practices. Near the top of the list should be their contribution to restoring the word *vocation*. In his book *The Call*, Os Guinness speaks of *calling* as meaning that "everyone, everywhere, and in everything lives the whole of life as a response to God's call."[2] He quickly points out, however, that this holistic and comprehensive view often gets distorted. The time leading up to Luther, as we just mentioned, was one of those instances of distortion. But as Guinness also points out, distortion comes at other times and in other places, too.

Certain pockets of contemporary evangelicalism revert to limiting *calling* to church work only. I remember, during college, interning in a youth ministry program. One of the adult lay leaders expressed to me how he wished he could do what I was doing, heading to seminary and preparing for a life of "full-time Christian work," as the saying goes. I remember thinking how he would benefit from a different perspective on his own life and work. He was an undercover state police officer—which greatly increased his "cool quotient" among the teens. He was a husband and a father to three daughters, and he was quite an active leader in the church. His impact was great, yet he had been conditioned to think that he was settling for something lesser, that his work wasn't as important as my future work would be.

I think what makes this story tragic is that it is no isolated story. Many, far too many, feel the same about their work. What is called for is a different perspective on work. Rightly understanding vocation can provide just the perspective we need.

The Reformers did us a great service by recovering the word *vocation*. Of course, we do them a disservice by thinking it's their special creation. As the Reformers put forth the doctrine of vocation, they were only articulating what they found to be true in Scripture concerning work. We can get an even broader and richer understanding of work by looking back, as they did, to what the Bible has to say on the matter.

WORKING THE GARDEN: A BIBLICAL AND THEOLOGICAL FRAMEWORK FOR WORK

The first place to look for a biblical and theological framework for work is in the beginning. Theologians have referred to Genesis 1:26–28 as the cultural mandate. As image-bearers, we are given the task of having dominion over and subduing the earth. A great deal has been said about how best to understand this text. The first challenge is grasping the idea of the image of God.[3] Some have pointed out that this should be understood substantively. The image of God is some sort of thing that we humans have that differentiates us from the rest of all created beings.

Others put forth the idea that the image of God is functional. Drawing on parallel ideas in other ancient Near Eastern cultures, those who hold this view point out that the mention of the image is sandwiched between commands to have dominion and subdue the earth. They further point out that in other ancient Near Eastern cultures and religious texts, kings were hailed as the image of their gods on earth, carrying out the duties of the gods. The term used to describe this is *vice-regent*. The kings were vice-regents.

In the creation narrative this is modified a bit. It's not simply a king who is vice-regent. Rather, all of humanity, both male and female (Gen. 1:27), is collectively functioning as the vice-regent. It's interesting to see how this theme is developed in the pages of Scripture. By the time we get to the end of the story at Revelation 22, we find that we are in the new heavens and the new earth, with the description in Revelation 22:2 looking a lot like the garden of Eden. Then we read in Revelation 22:5 that we "will reign forever and ever" with God and the Lamb. The purpose for which we were created will have come.

That's a quick look at the beginning and the end of the story. What happens in the middle, though, is also crucial. Of the many things occurring in the middle, two stand out. The first is the fall, Adam's fall, which is really the fall of all of us. That comes in Genesis 3. It has the effect of severing the ties that bound us to God, not to mention ill affecting the ties that bind us to each other and to the ground—to the earth itself (Gen. 3:14–19). The other standout item is the solution. The promised seed in Genesis 3:15, who turns out to be Christ our Redeemer, undoes what Adam did and reunites us to God and brings in the kingdom, the consummation of which is portrayed in Revelation 22:1–5.

What does this seeming excursion have to do with work, our subject at hand? The answer is: everything. This—the biblical story line of creation, fall, and redemption—is the theological framework in which we begin to understand our purpose in life. It is also the context through which we understand work as vocation. Without it, work is just work—just putting in time.

God's command to Adam and Eve to subdue and have dominion over the garden, to work the garden, is his creational purpose for humanity. We call this the *creation mandate* or the *cultural mandate*. God himself "worked" in creating—and he rested, too, but more on that later. Then he charged his special creation, humanity, to work in sustaining and cultivating his creation.

You'll notice the word *cultivation*. I find this word helpful in understanding the cultural mandate—the command to subdue and have dominion over the earth and its inhabitants. There are different ways in which one can subdue. You can subdue by beating into submission. But such an approach, while initially effective, can be counterproductive. The fact that this command was given in a garden, the garden of Eden, is instructive. You don't subdue a piece of land by beating it; this much I have learned from my Amish farmer neighbors. You subdue a piece of land by cultivating it. You cultivate it by supplying it with nutrients, by protecting it from erosion, and by giving it an occasional rest.[4]

It's not just farmers who can cultivate God's creation. We all can; in fact, we all are commanded to subdue and have dominion. We need to realize that the fall and the presence of sin in the world make this task difficult. None of us likes to admit it, but in our role as image-bearers, marred by sin, we can get it wrong. This is a fallen world—or, as Dietrich Bonhoeffer once put it, a fallen-falling world.[5] And we are fallen-falling creatures. But then comes the good news of redemption in Christ, and the concomitant readjustment of us as image-bearers. Though Adam blew it, and though we blow it, through Christ we can get it right.

Now we can see why the psalmist calls on God to establish the work of his hands (Ps. 90:17). Work is God's intention for us. He made us to work, and ultimately he made us to work for him. Let's not miss, either, the type of work that Adam and Eve were doing. It was physical labor, tending animals, tending the garden and its trees and vegetation.

As humanity has progressed and developed, work has expanded to entail all sorts of things. I spend hours at a keyboard—not at all the kind of work in which Adam and Eve engaged. But all of us are God's image-bearers, tasked with cultivating the particular piece of his garden in which he has placed us. We do this under the full sun of the realities of the fall. We sweat and we have thorns to deal with. (Being allegorical here, can computer viruses be likened to thorns?) But amid the sweat and the thorns, we are still commanded to work.

This theological framework raises work to a whole new horizon of understanding. As we think it through, we begin to see that in our work we are in the service of the King, making work both a duty and a wonderful privilege. We are not, harking back to Dolly Parton's lyric, merely rungs on the "boss-man's ladder." We are image-bearers of the King, tending his garden.

There's one further piece to this. If God designed us this way—and he did—then it makes sense that when we are doing what God made us to do, we will be fulfilled and satisfied and happy. Work, then, is far more than a duty; work can actually bring pleasure. It doesn't have to be the drudgery that it is so often painted as being.

I don't think this is a question of surrounding your workplace with inspiring slogans or having employee meetings with gurus presenting seminars on self-fulfillment by being a team player. Those techniques can become rather manipulative, turning workers into pawns. Instead, it's a matter of adopting a theological framework of what God is doing in the world and how you fit into the picture. And it's also a matter of applying that theological framework to your work, day in and day out, hour after hour.

What you do from 9 to 5 or whenever you work is not disconnected from your Christian life and walk. It is not somehow outside the parameters of things that are a service and are pleasing to God. Your work is squarely in the center of your devotion and service and even worship of God. Even work that now seems meaningless or trivial may come to have far greater significance. Many times it's only after the fact, as we reflect back on our lives, that we can see how God used us and our work for his glory.

This theological framework applies even if your work is for a company that treats you like a machine from which it can extract the most productivity possible. It applies in situations in which those above you have no such theological framework even remotely in place. It applies because ultimately we are accountable to God for all that we do.

There is one final piece to this theological framework of work, and it concerns rest. God himself set the pattern by working for six days to create the universe and then resting. The biblical teaching of God's method in creating probably has more to do with us than it does with God. Let me explain. God didn't need six days to create. He could have done it instantaneously. And he certainly didn't need to rest. Since

God is omnipotent, creation did not deplete him of even an ounce of energy.

What we may very well have in the creation account is a pattern for us, a pattern of work and rest. The pattern of work, God creating in six days, teaches us that things take time. Farmers prepare soil, sow seeds, and then harvest after a long wait. So it is with our work. Building and making things—especially things of substance and things of beauty— takes time. But there is also the pattern of rest. This comes at the end of the workday. And it comes at the end of the workweek. The discussion of the Sabbath in Exodus 20:8–11 draws directly from the creation week. Six days we are to work and on the seventh we are to rest: "For in six days the LORD made heaven and earth, the sea, and all that is in them, and rested the seventh day" (Ex. 20:11).

In the aftermath of the French Revolution, the seven-day week was supplanted by a ten-day week, as part of the program to rid France of its religious identity and tradition. One should say *attempted* to supplant, for it was a failure. We have our own version of attempting to supplant the Sabbath, as evidenced in the phrase 24/7. In our connected world, we are always available, always working, all day long, every day of the week. At the very least, a Christian should consider saying only 24/6. God has established a day of rest for us. We shouldn't think we are wiser than he. But even to say 24/6 may be pushing it. Machines work around the clock. People can't.

Many have pointed out that people nowadays, especially those of us in Western cultures, play at our work and work at our play. This is yet another way in which we have distorted the biblical pattern of work and rest. We have lost the true meaning of leisure, likely because we have lost the true meaning of work. Once again I look to my Amish neighbors. My Amish neighbors rather obviously enjoy themselves at rest. And I think they know how to rest so well because they know how to work so well.

In giving us the pattern of six days of work and a day of rest, God is teaching us to establish boundaries and to establish healthy rhythms of life. A colleague of mine at Lancaster Bible College recently moved some distance away from the college. He was finding, living so close, that he was there a great deal—at night, after a long day, and on the weekend. He and his family made this move in order to develop, in his words, "healthy rhythms of work, time for family, and rest."

Moving might be too drastic for you. But there is a lesson to be learned here. We can be influenced by the "24/7" or by the "work at play, play at work" cultural pariahs that plague us. We're not immune to these influences as Christians. Finding yourself checking your e-mail on Saturdays and Sundays, or during dinners with your spouse or family, can be a symptom of an unhealthy pattern of work. Rather, we need to pay attention to the boundaries that God has ordained for us. We need to be attuned to the healthy rhythms of work and rest.

There is more to the biblical teaching on work than the beginning in Genesis 1:26–28 and the end in Revelation 22:1–5. There is quite a bit in the middle. The Bible not only provides a frame for work, but also offers a great deal in terms of filling in the picture. We'll explore the contours of this picture in a moment. For now, though, it's helpful to think about how not to work. The negative can sometimes vividly point us to the positive. Learning how not to work, in other words, can be the first step toward learning best how to work.

HOW NOT TO WORK

In Oliver Stone's 1987 movie *Wall Street*, ruthless investor Gordon Gekko, played by Michael Douglas, delivers a speech on greed before the Teldar Paper shareholders at their annual meeting. Gekko is there to launch his takeover. "America has become a second-rate power," he tells fellow investors, pointing to greed as the answer. "Greed, for lack of a better word, is good. Greed is right," adding that greed in its raw and in its full essence marks the upward evolutionary climb. Then he crescendos, "Greed, you mark my words, will not only save Teldar Paper but that other malfunctioning corporation called the USA."[6] The Gordon Gekko "Greed is good" speech has become famous not only among the readers of *Forbes* magazine but also in broader reaches of culture as an American icon. The speech is, however, a classic case of art imitating life.

Any of the handful of high-profile corporate raiders arrested during the 1980s could have served as the inspiration and the template for the character. But it was Ivan Boesky who delivered a 1986 commencement speech at the University of California-Berkeley School of Business Administration and told would-be graduates that "greed is all right," adding, "Greed is healthy." The next year, just after the release of *Wall Street*, Boesky was sentenced to three and a half years in a federal prison and fined $100 million.[7]

The problem with such glaring examples as the fictional Gekko and the real-life Boesky is that they mask the less obvious and less glaring greed that operates in all of us at least some of the time, and in most of us more often than we'd like to admit. Of course, there is a difference between greed and ambition. Ambition can be a good thing. Employers like ambitious employees. Teachers like ambitious students. Parents like ambitious children. And pastors like a congregation of ambitious parishioners. But ambition can quickly get carried away with itself. The issue may be posed by asking, "Ambitious for *what?*" Christ clearly tells us to

seek first the kingdom of God (Matt. 6:33). If we are ambitious for anything else, we do things, even good things, for
all the wrong reasons.

For these reasons, ambition can easily turn into greed.
And greed, once it has run its course, consumes. We can work
very hard, which can be a good thing. But we can also easily
and quickly work very hard for the wrong reason, the reason
of self-advancement and self-promotion. The fictional Gekko
may be right after all. Greed marks the upward evolutionary
climb. It's just that for those who are disciples of Christ, the
law of the survival of the fittest, fueled by greed, is a lie—and
a damning lie at that.

The opposite of greed is one of the other deadly sins,
sloth. One of the most colorful, if not comical, descriptions of
sloth in the Bible comes from Proverbs 26:15: "The sluggard
buries his hand in the dish; it wears him out to bring it back
to his mouth." And this was written before we had christened
the couch potato. Here's a person who is so lazy that, once he
has put his hand in the dish, he hasn't the energy to bring it,
along with the food it grabbed, up to his mouth.

There are indeed as many glaring examples of laziness
in our culture as there are examples of greed. The remote
control, not to mention all the other technological gadgets
we have showered upon ourselves, reveal that if anything we
as a culture are against effort, against sweat, against work.
This laziness can affect our professions and our relationships. We want instant success, without work or any invest-
ment of time. We become conditioned to appreciate only easy
experiences and to dread the routines of hard work. These
cultural malpractices can spill over from our professional
and personal lives into our spiritual lives. On that score,
too, we can look for shortcuts to spiritual maturity. But such
looking is in vain.

Just as we need to point out that there is a difference between ambition and greed (though that line is indeed a fine one), so there is a difference between laziness and rest. Rest is healthy for us, even necessary. But habits of rest can easily and quickly become unhealthy. We have far too many couches and recliners at our disposal to avoid that temptation. Again, just as a healthy view of work can be overcome by ambition and then overcome by greed, so too our rest, which is both necessary and God-ordained, can be overcome by laziness and sloth. Whereas ambition is a race to the top, sloth is a race to the bottom. Both take us down the wrong path. Proverbs overflows with warnings about playing out this dance with greed and with sloth. And Proverbs wisely and distinctly shows how both partners lead to death and destruction.

It's worth contemplating these two ways of ambition and of laziness. Many people see these as the only two options of thinking about work. Either work becomes all-consuming or it is to be avoided at all costs. The solution lies not in finding a balance, but rather in thinking entirely differently about work and about rest. We saw this briefly in the biblical passages we considered above as we constructed a theological framework for work. It's time to turn once again to that framework, this time looking for practical application.

HOW TO WORK

In our technological culture, we find ourselves for the most part rather far removed from the things we wear and use and even eat. In cultures of the past, especially in ancient cultures of biblical times, there was much more of a connection between one's work and the fruits or products of that work. As we shifted from agrarian economies to industrial economies, that divide widened. As we shifted from industrial economies to our current technological economies, that gulf widened further still. This has had a net effect on our twenty-first-century sensibilities of making us think quite differently from people in previous centuries about work and products and about their value. Some of this has had a negative impact. We are numb to the factory conditions of foreign labor that produces the products we use and throw away. And we are numb to what happens to those products we throw away as they end up in landfills. These disconnects, so much a part of our consumer culture, cause us to lose touch with each other and with the world God has made.

We have a further disconnect when we consider the imbalanced scale of wages. Professional athletes earn more in a year than factory workers, who make the baseballs and basketballs and athletic shoes, earn in lifetimes of work. And let's not even mention other celebrities.

In light of these disconnects, it's all the more urgent that we think biblically and theologically about work. This is true for both employees and employers. Christians who find themselves in either role are under an obligation to think and live biblically at work.

One text that can help here is Ephesians 6:5–9. In this passage Paul is addressing slaves and masters. This can get complicated and has all too often been a source of misinterpretation. In an attempt to not misstep in this minefield, I will simply regard this passage as contributing something to what it means to be an employee and an employer. As for employees, Paul points out that they ultimately work for God. We are to render "service with a good will as to the Lord and not to man" (6:7). This relates directly to calling. When work is understood as a calling, it is understood as a calling from God. He is ultimately the One we work for.

This can be seen in some of the sculpture work in medieval architecture. Way up in the high reaches of the cathedral, just as much attention is paid to detail as in the sculptures down below at eye level. Now, no one could ever possibly see the fine details of the sculpture way up there. Cutting back on these details wouldn't have negatively impacted the soundness of the structure in any way, and you couldn't make an argument that it would have impeded the worship of those on the floor below. So why did the architects do it? Because they knew it was work in the service of God.

Much of what we do at work could be glossed over; much of what we do won't be scrutinized. (I find myself thinking this when I'm painting inside a closet, or weeding the flowerbeds behind my house.) We can all too easily coast through our work, caring very little about what we do. It is precisely at that point that Paul's words come into play. Our work, even the unseen or the less seen, is ultimately work before God.

My grandfather stepped away from the family business of a local newspaper and its print shops to work at Roebling Steel Company, along the Delaware River in New Jersey, as part of the home-front war efforts during World War II. The plant made steel cables, mostly for bridge construction. But during the war it made steel cables for tank tracks. It was complicated work—the steel could easily twist in the wrong way, becoming unusable. Due to the scarcity of resources during the war, incentives were offered to those who could skillfully untwist the steel and set it right. Soon my grandfather began to notice that workers around him were starting to twist the steel on purpose so that they could then fix it and receive the extra compensation. All that dishonesty didn't sit well with him at all.

There is a certain urgency to our lives. Maybe it is not quite the palpable urgency of wartime, but as people who work before God, we have a high and holy calling. Honest work done with integrity is the type of work that honors God and is fitting for the occasion. Dishonesty is all too easy and comes far too naturally. We need to guard against it.

This leads Paul to also say something about motives. We are to serve our employers with "a sincere heart" (Eph. 6:5). Motive is always a difficult test. We can very easily do the wrong thing for the wrong reason. It's marginally harder to do the right thing for the wrong reason. Hardest of all is doing the right thing for the right reason. God cares not only about the work that we do, but also about *why* we do the work that we do. Motive matters. Admittedly, right motives are hard to pull off every day and at every task. It's good to know that God is forgiving and gracious. But we shouldn't let the level of difficulty keep us from making the attempt.

Employees aren't the only ones with standards to live up to. Paul also has some things to say to employers. One is that employers need to live by the same code of right motives: "Masters, do the same to them" (6:9). It turns out that what is good for the goose is also good for the gander. Paul then adds, "Stop your threatening" (6:9). Manipulation and threats are not the way to run a company or to treat employees. The reason this is so, as Paul explains, stems from our equality before God. "There is no partiality with him" as he looks at employers and employees (6:9).

It's worth thinking about the principle here. In our consumer culture we have come to attach greater value to those who produce and consume more than to those who produce and consume less. We rank people according to their tax bracket. Paul, however, reminds us of the level ground that we all stand on.

Over in Colossians 3, the parallel text to Ephesians 6, Paul's advice on work may be summed up succinctly: "Whatever you do, work heartily, as for the Lord" (Col. 3:23).

Aside from Paul, the place where we probably learn the most about work is the book of Proverbs. Here we learn not only of the ways of the sluggard, but also of the type of work that honors God. Proverbs 16:3 commands, "Commit your work to the LORD," adding that "your plans will be established." This is one of the many helpful overarching principles offered in the book of Proverbs. It reminds us that God is at the beginning, the middle, and the end of our work. He is sovereign over our work, just as he is sovereign over all of his creation and creatures. This proverb is calling us to do nothing more than acknowledge what is already the case. This reminder is nevertheless necessary, for we often forget to do what comes as a natural result of acknowledging what is the case. We must honor God as the source and means and end of our work, because he is the source and means and end of our work.

Other proverbs delve into specifics. Many speak of the rewards of work. Proverbs 10:5 informs us that "he who gathers in summer is a prudent son," while conversely, "he who sleeps in harvest is a son who brings shame." A few chapters later, we find similarly that "whoever works his land will have plenty of bread, but he who follows worthless pursuits lacks sense" (12:11). And not to be missed is the rather direct approach taken in Proverbs 14:23: "In all toil there is profit, but mere talk tends only to poverty."

Proverbs also has a way of expressing this concept of reward on a much deeper level than the motive of profit. One proverb in particular stands out in this regard: Proverbs 12:14. Here we are told, "From the fruit of his mouth a man is satisfied with good, and the work of a man's hand comes back to him." The reward spoken of here is fulfillment, a satisfaction. Ultimately it's not a satisfaction that comes from accumulating wealth or the things that wealth buys.

It's a satisfaction that comes from fulfilling our purpose of working in service to God.

The author of Ecclesiastes picks up on this. There we are told, "Everyone should eat and drink and take pleasure in all his toil—this is God's gift to man" (Eccl. 3:13). Some take this to be sarcastic, believing that the author of Ecclesiastes is the most jaundiced and jaded person who ever lived. It's true that there is sarcasm in Ecclesiastes, but this text, coupled with various passages from Proverbs, seems to be pointing to something that is quite true. God has made us to work, and as we work we find contentment, satisfaction, and happiness. This is one of the many good gifts from God to us.

Returning to Proverbs, many of its teachings address the issue of skillfulness. Case in point is Proverbs 22:29, which states, "Do you see a man skillful in his work? He will stand before kings; he will not stand before obscure men." A similar idea is expressed in one of the psalms of Asaph concerning David. Asaph tells us that David "guided [Israel] with his skillful hand" (Ps. 78:72). We see other examples of skillfulness elsewhere in Scripture. Bezalel and Oholiab were skillful craftsmen who oversaw the design and construction of the tabernacle. These were people filled with "skill" and "craftsmanship" who devised "artistic designs" (Ex. 35:30–35). Bezalel and Oholiab were joined by many other "craftsmen in whom the LORD [had] put skill" for the work on the tabernacle (Ex. 36:1).

Here we learn that any skill we have is derived from God; he gives it to us. But even those who have been given gifts need to cultivate them. From time to time I have worked on home projects. We've remodeled bathrooms, put in wood floors, put up trim—all under the helpful instruction of my very skilled father-in-law. He can cut boards for a door or window frame and the finished product comes out perfectly square. I come under the school of thought whose motto is "Do your best, and caulk the rest."

There are some things I'm (somewhat) good at, and some things I'm not. God has given all of us gifts and has called us all to certain tasks. If we understand our work as calling, we will approach it like Bezalel and Oholiab and the many others as they built the tabernacle for God. We will do our work with skillful hands. And even when we're doing home projects we'll be reminded to do our work as unto the Lord.

The last piece of this biblical puzzle is to consider Christ and work. We turn here to the incarnation, where we see Christ as fully and truly human, as well as fully and truly divine. In his humanity Jesus took on certain roles. He was a son and a brother. He was even a citizen in an occupied state of the Roman Empire. And he was a carpenter's son and, presumably, a carpenter himself. In fully living in these roles, Christ demonstrates the value and integrity of the roles for us, and the value and integrity of our work. But more than this, Christ through his redemptive work undoes what Adam did in the fall. And he restores to us the ability and the capacity to be image-bearers as God intended us to be (see 1 Corinthians 15:42–49, along with 2 Corinthians 3:18 in its surrounding context).

As mentioned above, Dietrich Bonhoeffer referred to the world as a fallen-falling world. We may also say that it is a redeemed-redeeming world—that it is a world Christ has redeemed and through his church on earth is redeeming. As disciples of Christ and as image-bearers of both Creator and Redeemer, we can be instruments of the spreading of redemption. When we see our work, our calling, from this perspective, it is as if we have climbed high upon a mountain and can look out over the long and broad horizons of the meaning and value of our work.

We should not be surprised to find that Scripture has something to say about our work. In light of many wrong-headed notions about work encircling us from our cultural context, we should be quick to turn to its pages for guidance and direction. As we look to it, we begin to understand and appreciate vocation.

WORK AND PAYCHECKS

One last piece needs to be added to our consideration of vocation, and that is trying to delineate the issue of work and getting paid for work. Culturally, we have by and large attached work to a paycheck. The paycheck somehow legitimizes the time we spend on a task. Of course, paychecks are necessary; it's hard to shelter and feed ourselves and our families without them. But paychecks are not the sole factor in legitimizing work. And work done for a paycheck is not the only type of work there is. This especially has meaning for stay-at-home moms, the disabled, and the unemployed. To many in Western cultures, no one who falls under these categories truly works. That in itself shows the tyranny of the paycheck.

Our theology of work needs to be big enough to include work that isn't done for a paycheck. This not only helps correct wrongheaded thinking about those who don't receive a paycheck, but also helps those who don't receive a paycheck themselves. Christians who fit into these categories can, influenced by cultural pressures, at times lapse into thinking that their contributions are worth less than those who work for a paycheck. The doctrine of vocation has nothing to do with a paycheck, and therefore can be a great help to those who don't get one.

This can be especially true for the unemployed. What started out as a time of uncertainty for the American and global economy in the fall of 2008 not only has continued through 2009, but on many fronts has taken a further downward turn. For many, it is a time of general economic gloom. This current economic downturn, which some economists are saying will last for quite a while, has resulted in many job losses, shrinking retirement portfolios, and falling property values, leaving many on shifting if not sinking sands.

The economic downturn at the end of the 2000s may very well turn around. History does show, however, that economic cycles tend to wax and wane, leaving many who once were confident without such a secure place to stand. Even in good economies people face unemployment and financial setbacks. Those facing such circumstances are wise to seek counsel in terms of financial and personal survival. But in addition to such sage advice from experts, it's also helpful to think theologically about facing or dealing with unemployment.

First, great comfort can be taken in the doctrine of the sovereignty of God. God is not only sovereign, but also all-wise and all-good. He is, as theologians put it, omni-benevolent. This is no mere platitude. In fact, it is in the difficult moments when the doctrine of sovereignty may very well be most palpably felt and understood and appreciated. But it is also true that while God is sovereign, his purposes are quite mysterious to us—even confusing or confounding to us. Despite our difficulty in making sense of everything that happens in our lives, we still can take refuge in God's sovereign and good hand over our lives—a truth for the employed and unemployed alike.

Second, it may be helpful to think of ways in which one can still work even if unemployed. There are in fact many ways in which one can still work, and working can be quite healthy in such a circumstance, staving off downward spirals of self-doubt, self-pity, and even depression. Volunteer work for a church or community program can be a very rewarding use of time. Even time spent gardening, working in the soil with one's hands, can be a healthy experience during a challenging moment in life. Dealing with unemployment can be extremely difficult, a time that can be endured only by God's all-sufficient grace. But during that time one can still work and still find ways to fulfill the God-ordained calling to cultivate his garden.

Stay-at-home moms, the self-employed, the unemployed, the disabled, and even the employed—not to mention teachers and professors over the summers—can all face the temptation of slipping into unhealthy patterns of laziness. Turning to another movie of the 1980s might be helpful here. In the opening moments of *Mr. Mom* (1983), Michael Keaton's character Jack Butler gets downsized. At first he applies his energy to home projects and household chores. But as the weeks and months slip by he lets himself go, becoming hooked on soaps and junk food and looking very much like the sluggard from Proverbs. Humorous it may be on the screen. But it can slide off the screen and become true in real life, and then it becomes not so humorous.

God made us to work. To be sure, our own work can look very different from the work of others and people can work at different levels from each other. But all of us are to work, even if it isn't for a paycheck.

FINDING MEANING IN THE ORDINARY: DOING ALL TO THE GLORY OF GOD

Moses expresses the vision that this booklet has sought to lay out: "Let the favor of the Lord our God be upon us, and establish the work of our hands upon us; yes, establish the work of our hands!" (Ps. 90:17). Moses doesn't use the word *vocation* in this text. But the type of work that Moses is referring to here can be done only when work is viewed as a calling. God has called us to a variety of tasks, from the roles that we play to the kinds of work that we do. He has given us competencies and skill sets and gifts. And he desires that we use them all in the service of his glory. We are called to be husbands and wives, parents and children. We are called to be workers in his garden.

For some of us this takes the form of professional jobs; for others it means factory work; for others still it means never once receiving a paycheck. What holds all these various roles and types of work together is that they all entail routines. No matter how glamorous the work—an astronaut, for instance, or a mystery-novel writer—all work involves routines: the day-in, day-out, hour after hour of plodding along and plugging away. Even relationships boil down to routines—even our relationship to God. When we understand all these activities and functions as vocation, as a calling, we gain a perspective on work that raises us above limited horizons. The doctrine of vocation enables us to see our work, all our work, as a means by which we can serve, worship, glorify, and enjoy God.

God has not left us without direction when it comes to work. In the pattern of creation itself, God graciously teaches us the value of work, as well as the healthy rhythms of work and rest. By creating us in his image and charging us to subdue and have dominion over his creation, God gives us a mandate to serve him and reveals to us the purpose and meaning of work. By sending us the Redeemer, the God-Man, who was a son and a brother and a carpenter, God was filling the roles that we play and the work that we do with purpose and significance and integrity. Scripture offers us a theological framework, which when applied to work can transform the routines and otherwise meaningless cycles of work into sacred acts of worship.

When we find this kind of meaning in our work, we find something permanent, something that lasts beyond us. As we get older, we tend to think more and more about our legacy. For some, that legacy consists of an estate and wealth and companies and institutions. For others, that legacy consists of children and grandchildren and great-grandchildren. For some, these legacies can become idols, perversions of God's good gifts into objects for self-fulfillment or self-promotion. The psalmist asks clearly that God establish the work of his hands, that God make something permanent, something lasting.

The extent to which we see our work as a calling to serve and ultimately to glorify God will be the extent to which our legacy lasts. It may be a legacy absent of great wealth or hordes of descendants. It may even be a legacy that goes entirely unnoticed by succeeding generations. But it will be an established legacy nevertheless, a legacy of good and faithful labor done for the glory of God.

John Calvin once said, "Each individual has his own sort of living assigned to him as a sort of sentry post."[8] It is the place and the work to which God has called us. As Calvin continues, God asks of us but one thing: to be faithful stewards of the callings that he has entrusted to us and to be faithful stewards of our sentry posts. Culturally we are taught to rank these posts and callings—even to envy the posts and callings of others. We value and devalue people and their work, even ourselves and our own work, on these false scales and against false paradigms. From this false standard we wrongly evaluate our own work and worth, and the work and worth of others. The standard that works is the one that God has established.

"No task," Calvin tells us, "will be so sordid and base, provided you obey your calling in it, that it will not shine and be reckoned very precious in God's sight."9 The standard for evaluating our work and our worth is to see our work as a calling in the service of God, for his glory.

Paul says it clearly: "Whatever you do, do all to the glory of God" (1 Cor. 10:31). That certainly applies to our work. We should, like Johann Sebastian Bach, be able to attach two sets of initials to everything we do: our own initials and the initials SDG, *Soli Deo Gloria*. And as we do, we'll find that the words of the psalmist become true. We will find that God's favor is upon us, and that he is, by his grace and for his own glory, establishing the work of our hands.

NOTES

1 See Martin Luther, *Babylonian Captivity of the Church*, 1520; Stephen J. Nichols, *Martin Luther: A Guided Tour of His Life and Thought* (Phillipsburg, NJ: P&R Publishing, 2002), 82–84.

2 Os Guinness, *The Call: Finding and Fulfilling the Central Purpose of Your Life* (Nashville: Word, 1998), 31–32.

3 For views on the image of God, see Joe M. Kapolyo, *The Human Condition: Christian Perspectives through African Eyes* (Downers Grove, IL: IVP, 2005), 45–84.

4 My thinking here has been influenced by Wendell Berry. See *The Art of the Commonplace: The Agrarian Essays of Wendell Berry*, ed. Norman Wirzba (Washington, DC: Counterpoint, 2003).

5 Dietrich Bonhoeffer, *Works, vol. 3, Creation and Fall: A Theological Exposition of Genesis 1–3*, ed. John W. DeGruchy (Minneapolis: Fortress Press, 1997), 120.

6 12. "Greed Is Good," *Wall Street*, DVD, directed by Oliver Stone (1987; Beverly Hills, CA: Twentieth Century Fox Home Entertainment, 2000).

7 Quoted in Michael A. Santoro, *Profits and Principles: Global Capitalism and Human Rights in China* (Ithaca, NY: Cornell University Press, 2000), 36.

8 John Calvin, *Institutes of the Christian Religion*, 3.10.6.

9 Ibid.